Picnic Park

A Month by Month Sampler of Simple Pleasures

By Barbara Jones

Picnic Park

A Month by Month sampler of simple pleasures

By Barbara Jones

Editor: Donna di Natale
Designer: Kelly Ludwig
Photography: Aaron T. Leimkueler
Illustration: Lon Eric Craven
Technical Editor: Jeri Brice
Production assistance: JoAnne Groves

Published by:
Kansas City Star Books
1729 Grand Blvd.
Kansas City, Missouri, USA 64108

First edition, first printing
ISBN: 978-1-935362-52-4

Library of Congress Control Number:
2010938014

Printed in the United States of America by Walsworth Publishing Co., Marceline, MO

To order copies, call StarInfo at (816) 234-4636 and say "Books."

The Quilter's Home Page

www.PickleDish.com

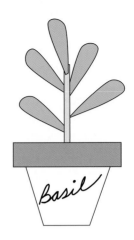

Basil

Dedication

For Merrell and Marie who took us on lots of picnics and to even more parades!

Acknowledgements

I would like to thank Catherine Timmons for her expert machine quilting and Jan Child for another beautiful and speedy binding. Both of these women work under impossibly tight deadlines and never drop the ball when it comes to meeting the schedule with quality workmanship. They make me look good and I am proud to think they are my friends. I would also like to thank Melinda Maw for sharing her sandwich recipe with me. She is the perfect combination of a "gifted-yet-humble" cook. I would also like to thank the folks at Kansas City Star Publishing. Their willingness to work with our fabric schedule made the job much easier. As always, I would like to thank the people of Henry Glass & Co for delivering the goods in time to make this book possible.

Note

Kits for Picnic Park in both fabric lines are available at www.quiltsoup.com while supplies last.

QuiltSoup patterns are available at www.quiltsoup.com.

For Summertime Fabrics and other QuiltSoup fabric collections, see: www.henryglassfabrics.com.

The Blocks

Single Flower Blocks
13

Single Tree Block
15

Double Tree Block
16

Big Watermelon Block
17

Picnic Basket Block
20

Tumbler Block
21

Flower Basket Block
22

Flower Pot Block
24

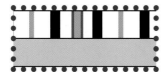

Pieced Block Sashes
25

Strip Pieced Sashes
27

About the Author

QuiltSoup is a quilt pattern and fabric design company owned and operated by Barbara Jones of Bountiful, Utah. Barbara has been a quilt maker for over twenty years, a quilt making teacher for ten years, and a business owner for the past six. QuiltSoup has produced over 60 patterns to date, two quilt books, and six fabric collections with four more on the drawing board. Their patterns have been published in several quilting magazines including *Quilts and More* and *The Quilt Sampler* (both by American Patchwork and Quilting), *The Quilters Companion*, *Australian Homespun*, and *QuiltMania*. *QuiltSoup*'s patterns and fabrics are distributed worldwide.

QuiltSoup specializes in beginner and intermediate appliqué patterns. "We love appliqué and want to spread the joy we find in it" says Barbara. "We teach beginning and intermediate classes both locally and nationally."

Please feel free to visit QuiltSoup's website www.quiltsoup.com and sign up for the free newsletter that features a new soup recipe each month. Check out the QuiltSoup blog anytime to see what's cookin'.

··· Introduction ···

Welcome to Picnic Park! It's a place to relax and hang out with friends and family. It is a place that is casual and filled with simple pleasures.

How did I get there? When I was girl, we didn't have central air conditioning, just a box fan. We later upgraded to a portable cooler. The cooler was this box shaped thing that we had sitting on a TV tray in the kitchen. You poured water into a reservoir in the cooler and the water dripped down while a fan blew air across the water to cool it. You had to refill the water all the time and it made the house humid. When it was really hot, my mother didn't want to heat up the house by cooking. Instead, our parents would take us to the park for a picnic under the shade trees. It always seemed to be a little cooler there. On weeknights, we might just take a tuna sandwich (which we always referred to as a tuna-fish sandwich...never just tuna), chips and soda to the park for our supper.

There were plenty of family reunions that included a summertime picnic in the park. Our standard picnic fare for the reunions was fried chicken, potato salad, baked beans, hard rolls, watermelon and Kool-Aid to drink. We also took a certain quilt with us on every picnic. We would spread it on the ground and sit on it while we ate our meal. It served as both a ground cover and tablecloth all in one. We still have this quilt and it goes to all the ballgames and summer outings that my mother attends. Often, someone at these reunions would bring a quilt to raffle off. The proceeds bought the watermelon and drinks for everyone at the reunion the next year. The real prize, though, was winning a quilt made by a favorite aunt or treasured cousin.

QuiltSoup's latest fabric collection for Henry Glass & Co. is called "Summertime". When I think of summertime I always think of those picnics and countless parades that I have been to. What better way to remember the picnics than with a quilt?

We designed this quilt with shade trees, a big watermelon and matching picnic basket, and flowers in baskets or pots -- or not. The blocks are presented in order of difficulty with the simplest being the first. We have updated the menu for the picnic with a recipe for a big sandwich that serves a crowd, keeps well in the heat and is easy to transport. I hope you will have as much fun stitching these blocks as I did. And if you raffle this one off, I hope you raise a ton of dough for the cause!

There are a few things you need to know before you start this project.

Terminology and icons:

* **Half square triangles (hst)** are squares that are cut once diagonally to yield two hst.

* **Pressing** is indicated by arrows over a seam. The arrowhead points in the direction in which to press the seam allowance.

* **Finished** and **cut** measurements are NOT the same thing.

* **Finished Measurement** means the size the block is after it is sewn into the quilt.

* **Cut measurement** means the size of the block before it is sewn into the quilt.

* **Over cut** means that the fabric for block is cut larger than the cut size. For example, we might "overcut" a block at 19 1/2" square; the "cut size" will be 18 1/2" square and the "finished size" will be 18" square. We overcut most appliqué backgrounds as there is some take-up that occurs during stitching. This allows you to appliqué, press and then trim the block down to the cut size. Think of it as a fudge factor. You will, however, need to keep all appliqué patches at least about 1" in from the margins of the overcut block.

* **Width of fabric (wof)** means from selvage to selvage. All measurements in this project are based on a wof of at least 42".

* **Mark and cut** means the patch is an appliqué patch. We first mark around the template on the right side of the fabric. This mark becomes the stitching line. We remove the template and cut the patch out adding a scant 3/16" seam allowance by eye as we go.

How we appliqué:

* You may work this pattern with any method of appliqué you prefer. If you chose to use fusible webbing you will want to reverse the appliqué patterns. We like to use the needleturn method so the templates given are designed for that method.

* This pattern is intended for those who are familiar with appliqué and is not an appliqué primer. We prefer needleturn appliqué for cotton patches. We use freezer paper instead of plastic for most of our templates. We like it because it is inexpensive, easy to cut accurately, stabilizes the fabric while you mark the stitching line and, we hope, it is better for the environment. Freezer paper has two sides -- a dull paper side and a shiny wax side. Prepare appliqué patterns by placing a piece of freezer paper over the pattern paper

side up. Trace the shape onto the freezer paper and cut it out on the line. Press the freezer paper pattern (shiny side down) onto the right side of fabric with a hot iron. Trace around the shape with a mechanical pencil on light fabrics or a white charcoal marker on dark fabrics. Cut the patch out by adding a scant 3/16" seam allowance by eye as you cut. Peel off the freezer paper. Glue-baste or baste patches in place. Keep patches at least 3/4" from all edges of background blocks as block edges are usually trimmed away. Appliqué patches. Press the back side first and then the front side. Trim block to size, if applicable.

- We use reverse appliqué in this project and have provided you with illustrations to explain what that is all about.

- We have also provided you with tips we have found useful, including an idea for aligning patches that overlap and underlap.

A word about borders:

Due to differences in skills and tools, your quilt center may vary from the ideal measurements by a little bit. We always recommend that you **measure your actual quilt center** before cutting borders to exact lengths. You may cut the border strips at the exact width but leave the piece about 2" longer than called for until you have measured your quilt. Cut to exact lengths after measuring. Measure horizontally through the center of your quilt to get the width and vertically to get the length.

Get yourself together:

It is important to stay somewhat organized when cutting this month by month quilt. I suggest you gather nine Ziploc bags. Label them with block names, e. g. Single Flower Block, Picnic Basket Block, etc. and label one "Borders and Sashes". Store your pre-cut pieces for each month in a separate bag. That way you won't cut up anything you should be saving! Label 5 more bags with the names of the colors and anything left over or called for in more than one block in these bags throughout the project. You will need a bag for: 1) black and gray, 2) red and peach, 3) green, 4) blue, and 5) white. I consider a scrap to be anything that is 2" square or larger. If you don't need the scraps, toss them at the end of the project.

Bag and tag:

To get the best use of your fabric and to be sure you don't cut up anything you will need later on, we will do a little pre-cutting and bagging.

Resources:

Fabric: "Summertime" by QuiltSoup for Henry Glass & Co. www.henryglassfabrics.com

A limited number of kits for this project are available from www.quiltsoup.com if your local quilt shop doesn't carry them. Please check with them first and always.

The Fabrics, Yardage & Pre-cutting Instructions

Batting 1 3/4 yards   **Backing 3 1/2 yards**

Black Texture — 1-3/4 yards:

* Cut 1 - 32" x wof strip and set aside for borders and sashes
* Cut 1 - 18" x wof strip and set aside for the flower blocks
* Cut 1 - 7" x wof strip and set aside for Single Tree and scraps

Black Floral — 1-1/8 yards:

* Cut 1 - 11" x wof strip and set aside for borders
* Cut 1 - 20" x wof strip. From this, cut 2- 20" squares. Set one aside for the Picnic Basket block. Cut the other one into 2 - 10" x 20" pieces. Set one of these aside for the Big Watermelon block. The other is a remainder.
* Cut 1 - 3 1/2" x wof strip for the Picnic Basket block.
* Use the remainders as needed.

Black Flowers and Baskets — 3/4 yards:

* No pre-cutting necessary

Grey Mini Dot — 1-1/8 yards:

* Cut 1 - 20" x wof strip and set aside for pieced sashes
* Cut 1 17" x 18" rectangle and set aside for the Flower Pot block
* Use remainder for the Picnic Basket block

White Stripe — 5/8 yard:

* Cut 1 - 11" x wof strip and set aside for borders
* Cut 1 - 4" x wof strip and set aside for strip pieced sashes
* Cut 1 - 5" x wof strip and set aside for tumblers and scraps.

White Lattice — 7/8 yard:

* Cut 1 - 14" x wof strip. Set aside for Single and Double Tree blocks.
* Cut 1 - 6" x wof strip. Set aside for the Picnic Basket block.
* Cut 1 - 5" x wof strip. Cut into 5" x 20" rectangles. Set one aside for the Tumbler Block and one for flower pot block.

Multi-Color Dots — 7/8 yard:

* Cut 1 - 11" x wof strip and set aside for border
* Cut 1 - 13" square for the Double Tree block
* Cut 1 - 5" x 20" for the Tumbler Block
* Use remainder as needed

Blue Squares – 3/8 yard:
* Cut 1 – 6" x wof strip and set aside for the Picnic Basket block.
* Use remainder for the Tumbler block and scraps

Green Squares – 7/8 yard:
* Cut 1- 4" x wof strip. Set aside for strip pieced sashes
* Cut 1 – 10" x wof strip. Cut into 2 – 10" x 21" rectangles. Set one aside for the Big Watermelon block.
* Use remainder as needed

Green Floral – 1/3 yard:
* Cut 1 – 5" x wof strip. From this cut 1 – 5" x 7" piece and set aside for the Tumbler block. Use the other part of this strip and the reminder as needed.

Red Squares – 2/3 yard:
* Cut 1 – 15" x wof strip. From this, cut 1 – 15" x 23" rectangle. Set aside for the Big Watermelon block.
* Cut 1 – 5" x wof strip. From this, cut 1 – 5" x 7" rectangle. Set aside for the Tumbler block. Use the rest of this strip for strip pieced sashes.

Red Floral – 3/8 yard:
* Cut 1 – 5" x 7" rectangle. Set aside for the Tumbler block. Use the reminder as needed.

Red Texture – 1-1/8 yards:
* Cut 1 – 16" x wof strip. From this, cut 1 – 16" x 23" rectangle. Set aside for the Double Tree block.
* Cut 1 – 19" x wof strip. From this cut 1 18" x 19" rectangle. Set aside for the Flower Basket block.

Peach Mini Dot – 1/2 yard:
* Cut 1 – 4" x wof strip. From this cut 1 4" x 23" strip and set aside for the Double Tree block. Use remainder for the Flower Pot Block.
* Cut 1 – 10" x wof strip. Cut strip into 2 – 10" x 21" rectangles. Set one aside for the Big Watermelon block. Use reminder for the Tumbler and Single Tree Blocks.

Notions:
* Template Plastic
* Freezer Paper
* Fine Point permanent marker
* Light and dark marking pencils
* 100% cotton thread to match appliqué patches
* Paper scissors
* Fabric scissors
* Appliqué scissors
* Roxanne's Glue-Baste
* John James Milliners, size 10 or 11

That Big Sandwich

*M*elinda Maw graciously shared this recipe with me. She made the sandwich for one of our quilting retreats. It is perfect for a crowd, easy to transport and keeps quite well in the heat. It can also be warmed in an oven if you prefer. It is pretty much an anything goes kind of sandwich.

- 1 loaf artisan French bread
- Assorted thinly sliced meats: prosciutto, Italian dry salami, ham
- Assorted cheeses: fresh mozzarella, provolone
- Garden tomatoes, thinly sliced
- Fresh basil, julienned
- Artichoke hearts, drained and chopped
- Dijon mustard
- Balsamic Vinegar
- Olive oil

The quality of the bread really makes all difference in this sandwich. We like to use an artisanal loaf from our local bakery. The outside is really crisp and the inside is kind of soft. It is worth the trip to the bakery for this one. Slice the French bread in half the long way so you have one big hoagie style loaf. Hollow out the center of each half by removing about half of the bread on the inside. Spread a thin layer of Dijon mustard on the inside of both bread halves. We usually scrape off most of the mustard before assembling the sandwich because not everyone loves it. We just want a hint of it in this sandwich.

Prepare a vinaigrette by mixing balsamic vinegar with a good olive oil in a 1:2 ratio. For example, 1/3 cup vinegar to 2/3 cup oil. You can use any proportions that you prefer and I frequently use about half vinegar and half oil. If you like Dijon mustard, you may also add it to this dressing. Of course you can shortcut this by using a bottle of your favorite vinaigrette from your local grocery store.

Drizzle a little dressing on the insides of both bread halves. Layer thinly sliced meat and cheese on bottom of sandwich. Go sparingly on the meat. The meats we always include are prosciutto, Italian dry salami and a good quality, thinly sliced ham. Other meats that are good with this are capricola, sopressata, and mortadella, but just use a little because they are spicy. The cheeses we use are provolone and/or fresh mozzarella. We like thick chunks of fresh mozzarella when the tomatoes are good and we have fresh herbs.

When the produce isn't as good we use fontina cheese and heat the sandwich in the oven.

Drain artichoke hearts completely. Chop. Layer on top of meat and cheese. You can include roasted red peppers and thinly sliced avocados if you like but take care that the whole thing doesn't get too slippery. We usually use just the artichoke hearts.

Layer thinly sliced fresh tomatoes next. Drizzle the dressing over this layer and repeat the layer. Place the meat and cheese on the second layer and then smash the sandwich down. Keep smashing and drizzling as you go. Top the final layer with lots of julienned fresh basil, a sprinkle of oregano and a few leaves of fresh salad greens. Drizzle and smash again. Drizzle dressing on the inside of the sandwich lid and place on sandwich. Smash the whole thing down again and wrap tightly with foil. Place in the frig with something heavy on top of sandwich to smash it down. Let it marinate for a few hours.

If you are warming the sandwich, leave the salad greens, tomatoes and basil off until the sandwich comes out of the oven. Drizzle the dressing and add the tomatoes basil and greens at the same time.

Tip: If you are using fresh basil from your garden, cut at least a 6-inch stem. Use the lower leaves in the sandwich, then root the stem in a glass of water to get a jump on the next planting.

Picnic Park

Finished size 55" x 69"

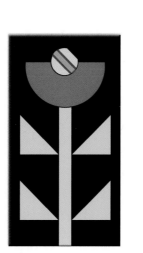

 # Single Flower Blocks

Finished sizes: 9" x 16" (Block 1) and 9" x 20" (Block 2) - Make 1 of each size

These flower blocks are primarily pieced and both are made almost the same way. They are cut to different heights after block sections are sewn together. Cutting is given for both flower blocks.

Cutting:

Black Texture: Cut 2 – 7 1/2" squares for top of block

Cut 4 – 4" squares for leaf area. Cut in half diagonally once to yield 8 half square triangles

Cut 2 – 3 5/8" x wof strip. From this, cut the following:

Cut 4 – 2 1/4" x 3 5/8" rectangles

Cut 4 – 2 5/8" x 3 5/8" rectangles

Cut 4 – 1 3/8" x 3 5/8" rectangles

Cut 4 – 1 1/2" x 18 1/2" strips for sides of block

Cut 1 – 2 1/2" x 9 1/2" strip for top of block 2.

Green Squares: Cut 2 – 4" squares. Cut in half diagonally once to yield 4 half square triangles

Green Floral: Cut 2 – 4" squares. Cut in half diagonally once to yield 4 half square triangles

Cut 2 – 1 1/4" x 11 1/2" strips for stems

Red Floral: Mark and cut 2 – flower heads

White stripe: Mark and cut 2 – flower centers

Assembly:

1. Sew green floral and black texture half square triangles into squares and press toward the black.

2. Sew green squares and black texture half square triangles into squares and press toward the black.

3. Green floral and green squares are alternated within the block and are opposite from one block to the next. Clear as mud? See if this helps. The diagram shows black only on the half square triangles which we are focusing on in this illustration.

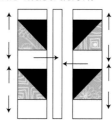

4. Sew left hand leaf panel together in the following order and press toward rectangles.

   a. Black 1 3/8" x 3 5/8" rectangle

   b. Green floral half square triangle

   c. Black 2 1/4" x 3 5/8" rectangle

   d. Green squares half square triangle

   e. Black 2 5/8" x 3 5/8" rectangle

5. Sew right hand leaf panel together in this order and press to rectangles.

   a. Black 1 3/8" x 3 5/8" rectangle

   b. Green squares half square triangle

   c. Black 2 1/4" x 3 5/8" rectangle

   d. Green floral half square triangle

   e. Black 2 5/8" x 3 5/8"rectangle

6. Sew 1 - 1 1/4" x 11 1/2" stem between left and right leaf panels. Press toward stem.

7. Sew 7 1/2" black square to top of stem/leaf unit and press toward the square.

8. Repeat these steps for the second flower block but change the placement of the green fabrics as follows:

   Left hand leaf panel

   • Black 1 3/8" x 3 5/8"

   • Green squares half square triangle

   • Black 2 1/4" x 3 5/8"

   • Green floral half square triangle

   • Black 2 5/8" x 3 5/8"

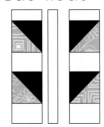

   Right hand leaf panel

   • Black 1 3/8" x 3 5/8"

   • Green floral half square triangle

   • Black 2 1/4" x 3 5/8"

   • Green squares half square triangle

   • Black 2 5/8" x 3 5/8"

9. Sew black 1 1/2" x 18 1/2" strips to both sides of both flower blocks. Press toward these strips.

10. Position red floral flower heads slightly over the top of the stem and within the 7" square at the top of the block. Position striped flower center over flower and appliqué both in place.

11. Trim Flower Block 1 to 16 1/2" high by cutting 1/2" from bottom of block and 1 1/2" from top of block.

12. Do not trim Flower Block 2. It is the taller of the two blocks. Instead, sew a 2 1/2" x 9 1/2" rectangle to top of block and press to this strip.

Tips:

• *We have not overcut the backgrounds in this case. This means the block will be the size we need with no margin for trimming. We try to use this method when there are only a couple of patches that must be appliquéd in place so that the block is less likely to become distorted. We try not to handle these blocks any more than necessary to keep raveling to a minimum.*

• *Black texture: To orient the pattern the same direction on the half square triangles, cut half of the squares with the ruler in one direction and the other half with ruler turned 90 degrees.*

 Single Tree Block

Finished size: 12" square - Make 1

What would a picnic be without shade trees? Picnic Park has several trees to picnic under. The single tree block uses the medium size tree templates

Cutting:

White Lattice	Cut 1 – 13 1/2" square for block background. This is overcut and is trimmed to a 12 1/2" square after appliqué and pressing.
Peach Mini Dot	Mark and cut 1 Tree Canopy 1
Red Floral	Mark and cut 1 Tree Canopy 2
Black Texture	Mark and cut 1 Tree Trunk

Assembly:

1. Position canopy pieces on background first and glue-baste in place. This tree fills the space almost completely so be sure to stay within 3/4" of each side of the background block.

2. Position trunk over canopy. Again, be careful that bottom of trunk does not extend below 3/4" from the bottom of the background.

3. Appliqué canopy 1, canopy 2 and tree trunk, in that order.

4. Press. Trim block to a 12 1/2" square.

 *Double Tree Block*

Finished size 21" x 16" - Make 1

The Double Tree block is made much like the Single Tree block but has a peach strip that serves to ground the trees. Use the large and small tree templates for this block.

Cutting:

Red Texture: Cut 1 - 22 1/2" x 15" rectangle for block background

Peach Mini Dot: Cut 1 – 221/2" x 3" rectangle for bottom of block background

White Lattice: Mark and cut 1 Large Tree Canopy 1

Multi-color Dot: Mark and cut 1 Large Tree Canopy 2

Green Squares: Mark and cut 1 Small Tree Canopy

Black Flowers & Baskets: Mark and cut 1 Large Tree Trunk

Black Floral: Mark and cut 1 Small Tree Trunk

Assembly:

1. Sew 3" peach strip to bottom of red texture background and press seam open.

2. Position patches and glue-baste in place. The peach strip finishes at 2" so use the seam line as a guide for tree trunk placement. The large tree stands behind the small tree.

3. Appliqué in this order:

   a. Canopy 1 - large tree

   b. Canopy 2 - large tree

   c. Trunk - large tree

   d. Canopy - small tree

   e. Trunk - small tree

4. Press. Trim block to 21 1/2" wide x 16 1/2" high.

Tips:

1. *When trimming the block down to size lay the 2 1/4" inch line of your ruler on the seam line between the peach strip and the red background. Trim away the peach that extends beyond ruler.*

2. *In general, trim parallel sides of block first and then trim in the other direction making sure that you have 90 degree corners on your blocks. We find a 20 1/2" square Omigrid ruler to be invaluable for trimming appliqué blocks down to size. We always thought they seemed expensive so didn't buy one for a number of years. Now we know that they are soooooooo worth the money!*

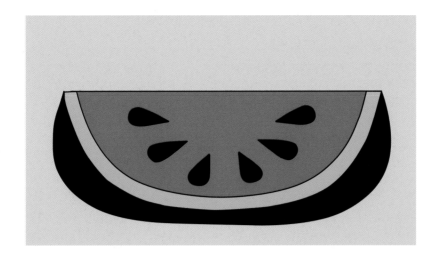

 ·· *Big Watermelon Block* ··

Finished size 21" x 12" - Make 1

This block requires several large templates. We recommend making them from freezer paper. Trace the melon patterns onto the dull side of the freezer paper and cut out on the drawn line. Make three complete patterns, one for each of the three melon shapes. Place the paper patterns on top of the right side of the fabric and press in place with a hot iron. The paper will stick to the fabric. Mark the stitching lines except at the top edge. Place a ruler on the marked line at the top edge of each pattern while it is still stuck to the fabric. Trim 1/2" beyond the marked line to give yourself a little wiggle room when aligning the melon patches with one another. Cut the rest of the melon out adding a 1/4" seam allowance by eye as you go.

Cutting:

Red squares:	Cut 1 – 13 1/2" x 22 1/2" rectangle for block background. This is an overcut and is trimmed down to 12 1/2" x 21 1/2" once appliqué and pressing are complete.
Black Floral:	Mark and cut 1 Melon 1
Green Squares:	Mark and cut 1 Melon 2
Red Texture:	Mark and cut 1 Melon 3
Peach Mini Dot:	Mark outside edges only and cut 1 Melon 3

Tips:

1. *Sewing order:*

   a. We are going to work this block in a different stitching order because the pieces are large. That means you may comfortably stitch a unit together in your hands before you stitch the unit to the background. It will also let you try working from the top down instead of from the bottom up. Prepare a separate full size template for each part of the watermelon. You will use more fabric than if you just overlapped the seam allowances of each patch. The ease of alignment is worth the extra fabric in my opinion.

   b. Notice that the templates for the watermelon include an extra large seam allowance. Use a 1/2" seam allowance on the top edge of this block until you reach the very last step. It helps you align the melon patches but leaves you enough room to trim down to an appropriate seam allowance right before you place the watermelon unit on the background.

Reverse appliqué:

a. We are reverse appliquéing the seeds onto the watermelon. What do we mean by that? Reverse appliqué simply means you reveal the shapes underneath the top layer instead of appliquéing shapes over the top layer.

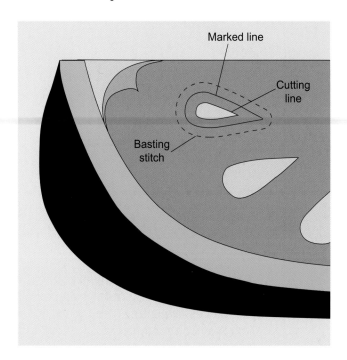

b. Why would we ever want to use reverse appliqué? Reverse appliqué is a technique that lets you execute tiny shapes that occur within a larger patch. For example, appliquéing very small berries about 1/4"-3/8" in diameter can be quite a challenge. You must fit a seam allowance under the berry all the way around the outside edge which creates a lot of bulk to manage. If you reverse appliqué the berries, you are distributing the seam allowance that you turn under over a larger area which helps your work lie flatter.

Assembly:

1. Reverse appliqué the seeds. Cut away inside the seed area marked on the watermelon (Melon 3) leaving a 1/8" seam allowance to turn under. Checkered area of illustration indicates the fabric to remove.

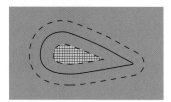

2. Place the peach fabric you cut for seeds under the red watermelon fabric, right sides up. Lightly glue-baste the pieces together but avoid gluing where the seeds will be. Baste about 1/4"-3/8" around the outside of each marked seed. This anchors both layers but leaves room to turn the seam allowance under. It also provides a line on the back of the fabric that shows you where to trim away.

3. When the watermelon fabric is laid over the top of the seed fabric it will look something like this. The marked line is the stitching line. Clip watermelon patch around the inside curve before stitching. Clip once at point of seed before stitching.

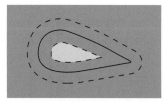

4. Appliqué by turning the seam allowance under and stitching as usual. The complete seed will be revealed. Reverse appliqué all 6 seeds.

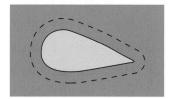

5. Cut away the excess seed fabric. Before you remove the basting, turn the work to wrong side. The basting line serves as a guide for cutting away excess fabric. Before you cut away, release any glue

holding the seed fabric and watermelon together. Cut away all fabric that extends beyond the basting. Remove the basting. Press unit.

6. Align the top of the melon/seed unit with the top of the rind. Glue-baste. Beginning at the side of the watermelon, appliqué the melon unit to the rind. Stop stitching when you reach the end of the other side of the melon. Do not appliqué the top edge. Turn work to the wrong side and cut away the excess rind fabric which under laps the center of the melon/seed unit.

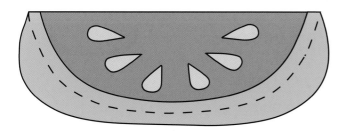

7. Align the top of the melon/seed/rind unit with the top of the black floral melon piece. Glue-baste. Beginning at the side of the watermelon, appliqué the melon/rind unit to the lower melon. Stop stitching when you reach the end of the other side of the melon. Do not appliqué the top edge. Turn work to the wrong side and cut away the excess black fabric which under laps the center of the melon/rind unit.

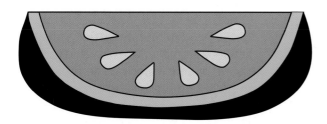

8. Mark the top stitching line on the right side of the work and trim seam allowance to a scant 1/4". Fold the melon in half vertically to find the

center and finger crease. Do the same thing with the background fabric. Place watermelon on background aligning the center creases. The bottom of the melon is placed about 2 1/4" up from the bottom of the background.

9. Appliqué the watermelon in place. Press.

10. Trim block to 21 1/2" x 12 1/2".

Tips:

When to consider cutting away from behind appliqué patches:

* *Multiple layers of fabric that add unacceptable bulk*

* *Dark background shadowing through and muddy-ing up the colors.*

How you get into trouble:

* *Before cutting into the piece you want to remove the extra fabric; let's call it the background in this example. To do this, stick the tips of your scissors into the background only. Lift the fabric up to be sure you just have the background fabric and not the appliqué patch. You can do this with a pin or needle as well. Make a small clip in the background and start cutting away. As soon as you have a hole big enough to put your finger into, pull the pieces apart gently, releasing any glue that may be holding the front and the back together. Continue doing this as the hole becomes larger. If the fabrics are separated from one another, you reduce the chances you will cut into the appliqué patch. There are special scissors in the marketplace to avoid cutting through your top patch. If you have them, by all means use them. I don't own a pair of these and cut away with my small appliqué scissors. I have only cut into the wrong layer once and once was enough! I was in a hurry, didn't separate the layers properly, and paid the price!*

 **Picnic Basket Block:**

Finished size: 17" x 16" - Make 1

*N*ow that you know how to reverse appliqué, let's try it again with a smaller shape!

Cutting

Black Floral:	Cut 1 – 18 1/2" wide by 17 1/2" high rectangle for block background
	Mark and cut 1 watermelon shape.
Black Texture:	Mark and cut 1 rivet for basket handle
Blue Squares:	Cut 1 – 15 1/2" x 4 3/4" rectangle for top of basket
	Cut 1 – 15 1/2" x 2 1/2" rectangle for basket bottom
Gray Mini Dot:	Cut 2 – 15 1/2" x 1" for stripes in basket
	Mark and cut 1 basket lid
White Lattice:	Cut 1 – 15 1/2" x 5 5/8" for watermelon background
	Mark and cut 1 basket handle
Red Texture:	Mark and cut 1 watermelon. Mark seed placement as well.
Green Floral:	Mark and cut 1 watermelon rind.

Assembly:

1. Reverse appliqué the seeds the same as for the watermelon block but using black floral fabric for seeds.

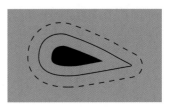

2. Press.

3. Appliqué red melon to green rind. Center the watermelon slice on the 15 1/2" x 5 5/8" white lattice strip and appliqué in place. Press well. Place the 1" line of your ruler on the top edge of the stitched melon and cut away the fabric beyond the ruler. Trim width to 4 5/8" Do not trim anything from 15 1/2" measurement for now.

4. Sew basket strip together in this order and press seams open.

   a. Blue squares: 4 3/4" x 15 1/2"

   b. Gray: 1" x 15 1/2"

   c. Melon strip: 4 5/8" x 15 1/2"

   d. Gray: 1" x 15 1/2"

   e. Blue squares: 2 1/4" x 15 1/2"

5. Cut the complete picnic basket bottom from the pieced panel by making a freezer paper template of the picnic basket bottom. Mark the lines for the narrow gray strips across template. Align these with the gray fabric when you place the template on the fabric. Mark and cut, adding a 1/4" seam allowance by eye as you go.

6. Place bottom of basket about 1 1/2" up from bottom of background fabric and centered on background rectangle. Place lid, then handle, then rivet over basket.

7. You will want to decide whether to cut away the background fabric from behind the picnic basket or not. If so, appliqué the basket to the background then cut away, leaving at least 1/4" seam allowance inside the basket. Next, stitch the lid, handle and rivet in place. The sewing order is the same whether you cut away or not. Be careful to cut only the background fabric away and not clip into all of your hard work!

8. Press and trim block to 17 1/2" wide by 16 1/2" high.

Tip: It is sometimes easier to assemble a complete appliqué shape before placing it onto the background. This is particularly true when the background is a dark fabric like the one used for this block. Lay appliqué patches over paper pattern to aid with placement. Glue baste the basket pieces together where there is overlap. Position the complete basket with handle onto the background.

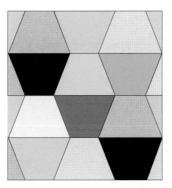

  *Tumbler block*

Finished size: 12" x 16" - Make 1

I suspect we will serve a beverage at the picnic which makes me think of those disposable plastic tumblers you can use for the outdoors. The Tumbler block is a good place to gather up a sampling of your leftover fabrics. Each piece is cut separately using a plastic template. Template A is for the tumblers and spacers and templates B and B reverse are for the sides of the block.

Tip: We cut directly around these templates with a rotary cutter. If this makes you too nervous, place the template right side up on the right side of the fabric and trace around it with a pencil. Cut the patch out trimming away the marked line as you cut.

Cutting:

Blue Squares	Cut 2 - A
	Cut 1 each B and B reverse
White Lattice	Cut 2 - A
	Cut 2 - B reverse
Multi-color Dot	Cut 2 - A
	Cut 1 - B reverse
Peach Mini Dot	Cut 1 each B and B reverse
Black Floral	Cut 2 - A
Red Squares	Cut 1 - A
Green Floral	Cut 1 - A

White Stripe	Cut 1 – A
	Cut 1 – B
Red Floral	Cut 1 – A

Assembly:

1. Patches are sewn together into 4 rows and all are pressed toward the darker fabric. When sewing tumbler patches into a row, use the trimmed corner angles to line up the patches correctly. Rows 1 and 3 contain 1 dark A patch. Rows 2 and 4 contain 2 dark A patches. Think of the dark patches as the tumblers and the light patches as spacers between them.

Rows 2 and 4

B reverse   A   A   A   B

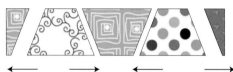

2. Sew rows 1 and 2 together and press seam toward row 1.

3. Sews rows 3 and 4 together and press seam toward row 3.

4. Sew these together into a block and press the seams up.

Rows 1 and 3

B   A   A   A   B reverse

Flower Basket Block

Finished size: 15" wide x 16" high - Make 1

When I asked my husband what flower baskets and pots had to do with a picnic, he said that anyone who knew me knew I would be bringing flowers for the table. I thought it would be fun to put those flowers into an old picnic basket to continue the theme!

Cutting:

| Red Texture: | Cut 1 - 16 1/2" x 17 1/2" rectangle for background. This is an overcut and will be trimmed to 15 1/2" x 16 1/2" after appliqué and pressing are completed. |

Black Flowers & Baskets: Mark and cut 1 basket bottom and 1 basket handle

Peach Mini Dots: Mark and cut 1 left and 1 right flower

White Stripe: Mark and cut 1 left and 1 right flower centers

Green Floral: Mark and cut 1 right stem

Mark and cut 1 left stem and 1 leaf 2

Green Squares: Mark and cut 1 leaf 1 and 1 leaf 3

Blue Squares: Mark and cut 1 leaf 4

Multi-color dot: Mark and cut 1 each of berries 1-5. Note that they are all different sizes. I fussy cut them from the fabric by positioning the polka dot slightly askew on each berry. I cut berries 1, 3 and 4 with a blue dot in the center and berries 2 and 5 with a light gray dot in the center.

Assembly:

1. Appliqué in the following order:
   a. Basket handle
   b. Stems
   c. Basket
   d. Leaves
   e. Berries
   f. Flowers
   g. Flower Centers

2. Press and trim block to 15 1/2" wide by 16 1/2" high.

Tips:

Many of the patches in this block overlap or under-lap other patches. You can handle placement of these patches in a couple of ways.

1. *This is the method I use and recommend. Mark the intersection of patches that overlap with a pencil hash mark in the seam allowance. Match these hash marks when over or under-lapping. Once the appliqué is completed, no one ever see these marks and they are very helpful for positioning patches.*

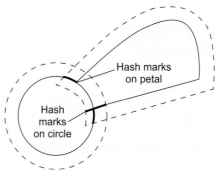

Hash marks on petal

Hash marks on circle

2. *Alternatively, make a paper pattern of the complete block by photocopying the diagrams in the book and then aligning the dashed lines that indicate the page. Tape the pages together and place the pattern on a light box. Place background fabric over the pattern and lightly tape the sides in place with a tiny piece of tape. Position the patches and glue-baste in place. Work from the deepest or bottom part of the design up to the top piece. In this case, the deepest part of the design is the basket handle then the stems, etc. as listed in the assembly order.*

3. *Relax a little bit! We don't do anything so precise that positioning is critical. We place patches where we think they look good to us. That might be a little different from where you like them. The most important things about positioning the patches is that they are recognizable as the shape they should be (a flower with its stem) and that all pieces are at least 3/4" inside the margin of the background to allow for trimming and sewing the block.*

 *Flower Pot Block*

Finished size: 15" x 16" - Make 1

sometimes take potted plants to a picnic instead of or in addition to the flowers. A potted herb is a nice giveaway for guests. We are using basil in our picnic sandwich so we thought it would be fun for picnic goers to take a little basil cutting or plant grown from seed home with them. You can whitewash a terra cotta pot and then paint, print or write the name of the herb on the pot. You can plant the same kind for each guest or do a variety of different herbs. If you are like me, you won't think of this until the day before the picnic. Plant them anyway! Although the herbs won't have sprouted yet, the thought and gesture will still be the same!

Cutting:

Gray Mini Dot:	Cut 1 - 16 1/2" x 1717 1/2" rectangle for block background. This is an overcut and will be trimmed to 15 1/2" x 16 1/2" after appliqué and pressing.
White Lattice:	Cut 1 - 4" x 14" strip for top of pot
Red Texture:	Cut 1 - 1 1/4" x 14" strip for middle of pot
Peach Mini Dot	Cut 1 - 3 1/2" x 14" strip for bottom of pot
	Mark and cut 1 flower head
Red Floral	Mark and cut 2 flower heads

Black Texture	Mark and cut 1 left, center and right stem
Black Floral	Mark and cut 1 leaf 1
Blue Squares	Mark and cut 1 leaf 2
Green Squares	Mark and cut 1 leaf 3
Green Floral	Mark and cut 1 leaf 4
Black Flowers & Baskets	Mark and cut 1 leaf 5
Multi-color Dot	Mark and fussy cut 3 flower centers. The centers are 1 1/2" diameter circles. I centered the dot in the circle which left a white margin about 1/8" all the way around the outside of the dot.
	Mark and cut 1 pot foot.

Assembly:

1. Flower Pot:

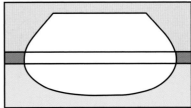

The flower pot is strip pieced. Make a freezer paper template for the complete pot. Mark the placement of the stripe on the bowl on the template. Sew the 1 1/4" x 14" strip of red texture between the 14" white lattice and peach mini dot strips. Press seams open. Place freezer paper template, dull side up, on the right side of the pieced unit with the stripe marks aligned with the red texture strip in the middle of the unit. Press to adhere. Mark around the outside of the pot template. Cut the pot out adding a scant 1/4" seam allowance by eye as you go.

2. Position the pot foot in the center of the block and aligned with the bottom edge of the overcut background. You will appliqué only the sides of the pot foot.

The bottom will be caught in the seam allowance. The top will be covered by the pot.

3. Place stems, leaves, flowers and pot onto background and glue baste in place.

4. Appliqué in the following order:

   a. Pot foot

   b. Stems

   c. Pot

   d. Leaves

   e. Flower circles

   f. Flower heads

5. Press and trim block to 15 1/2" x 16 1/2".

Sashes

There are four pieced block sashes and two strip pieced sashes in this quilt. Cut and sew all of the sashes before you start to assemble the quilt.

Pieced Block Sashes

There are four pieced block sashes in this quilt. The center row of each of these sashes is strip-pieced and varies only in the length. Cutting is given for all 4 pieced block sashes. Make 1 of each.

* Sash 1 finishes at 4" x 16"

* Sash 2 finishes at 4" x 33".

* Sash 3 finishes at 4" x 36"

* Sash 4 finishes at 4" x 45"

Cutting:

Black texture: Cut 4 – 2 3/4" x wof strips for strip pieced portion of sash

Gray Mini Dot: Cut 7 – 1 3/8" x wof strips. From these, cut:

   * 4 – 1 3/8" x 36 1/2" strips,

   * 2 – 1 3/8" x 33 1/2" strips, and

   * 2 – 1 3/8" x 16 1/2" strips for outside edges of sashes.

   From the remainders cut:

   * 3 – 1 3/8" x 2 3/4" rectangles and

   * 1 – 1 5/8" x 2 3/4 for ends of sashes.

   Cut 4 – 2 1/4" x wof strips for strip pieced portion of sash.

   Cut 1 – 4 1/2" x 9 1/2" rectangle for left hand end of sash 4.

Assembly:

1. Sew black texture 2 3/4" x wof strips and gray 2 1/4" x wof strips into pairs. Press to the black. Cut segments from this strip set that are 2 3/4" wide as shown in illustration.

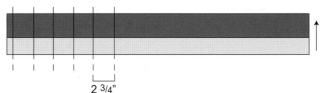

2. Sew segments together as shown for each sash. Trim the last gray rectangle to the measurement given for each sash. Sew a gray strip to the left hand end of each strip as listed. Press to the black. Sew gray 1 3/8" x given length to top and bottom of pieced sections. Press to gray.

Sash 1   4 1/2" x 16 1/2"

* Top and bottom gray strips: 1 3/8" x 16 1/2"

* Right hand rectangle: Trim to 1 1/8" wide

* Left hand gray rectangle: 1 3/8" x 2 3/4"

Sash 2   4 1/2" x 33 1/2"

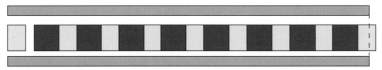

* Top and bottom gray strips: 1 3/8" x 33 1/2"

* Right hand rectangle: Trim to 1 3/8" wide

* Left hand gray rectangle: 1 5/8" x 2 3/4"

Sash 3   4 1/2" x 36 1/2"

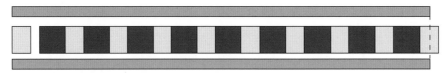

* Top and bottom gray strips: 1 3/8" x 36 1/2"

* Right hand rectangle: Trim to 1 1/8" wide

* Left hand gray rectangle: 1 3/8" x 2 3/4"

Sash 4   4 1/2" x 45 1/2"

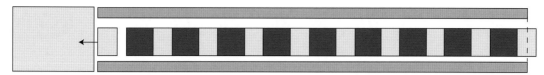

* Top and bottom gray strips: 1 3/8" x 36 1/2"

* Right hand rectangle: Trim to 1 1/8" wide

* Left hand gray rectangle: 1 3/8" x 2 3/4"

* Left hand big rectangle: 4 1/2" x 9 1/2

Strip Pieced Sashes

Cutting

White stripe:	Cut 1 - 1 1/2" x 12 1/2" strip for sash A beneath row 2
	Cut 1 - 1 1/2" x 30 1/2" strip for sash B beneath row 3
White Lattice:	Cut 1 - 1 1/2" x 33 1/2" strip for sash A beneath row 2
Green Squares:	Cut 1 - 2 1/2" x 30 1/2" strip for sash B beneath row 3.
Red Squares:	Cut 1 - 3 1/2" x 15 1/2" strip for sash B beneath row 3.

Assembly

Sash A

* Sew 1 1/2" x 12 1/2" white stripe to 1 1/2" x 33 1/2" white lattice and press toward stripes.

Sash B

* Sew 1 1/2" x 30 1/2" white stripe rectangle to 2 1/2" x 30 1/2" green squares rectangle and press to green.

* Sew this unit to 3 1/2" x 15 1/2" red squares rectangle and press away from red squares.

Row 1:

Sew Picnic Basket block to 16 1/2" high Single Flower block. Press to Picnic Basket. Sew Sash 1 to the right hand side of the Flower Basket block. Press to sash. Sew blocks into a row. Press toward Flower Basket block.

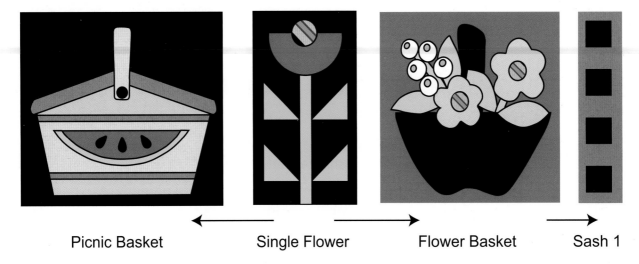

Picnic Basket   Single Flower   Flower Basket   Sash 1

Row 2:

Sew Single Tree block to Watermelon block. Press toward Watermelon block. Sew Sash 2 to top of this unit and press to sash. Sew Tumbler block to right hand side of this section. Press away from Tumbler block. Sew Sash A to bottom of this row and press toward Sash A.

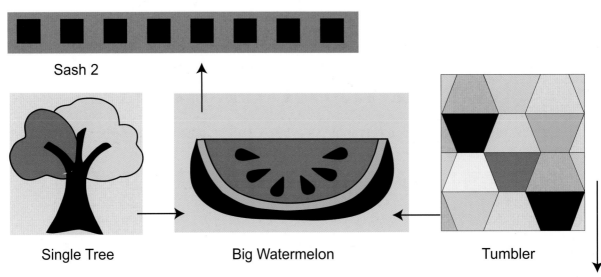

Sash 2

Single Tree   Big Watermelon   Tumbler

Sash A

Row 3:

Sew Flower Pot block to Double Tree block and press toward trees. Sew Sash 3 to top of these blocks and press to sash. Sew 20 1/2" tall Single Flower block to right hand side of this section. Press toward Single Flower block. Sew this double sash unit to the bottom of row 3 and press toward sashing.

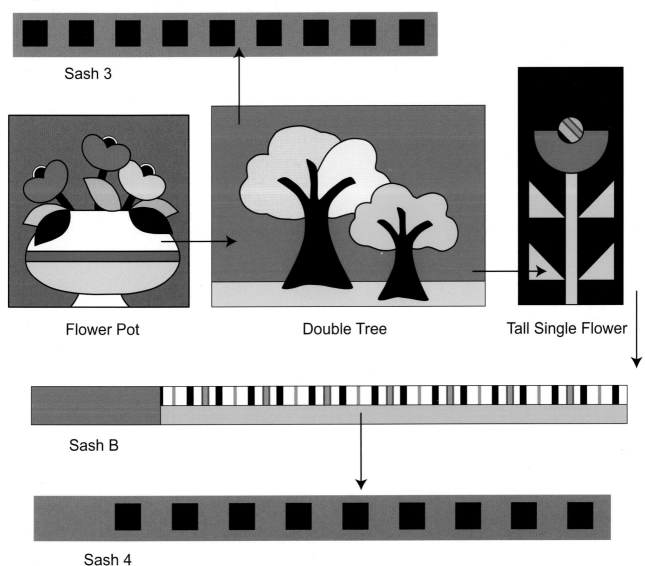

Sash 3

Flower Pot   Double Tree   Tall Single Flower

Sash B

Sash 4

Sew rows 1-3 together in order.

Cutting:

Black texture: Cut 4 – 2" x wof strips for left and top inner borders

Cut 2 – 4 1/2" x wof strips for right hand border

White stripe: Cut 2 – 4 1/2" x wof strips for left hand border

Black Floral: Cut 2 – 4 1/2" x wof strips for bottom border

Multi color dot: Cut 2 – 4 1/2" x wof strips for top border

Assembly:

1. Left hand inner border:
   Sew two of the black texture 2" strips end-to-end to make one continuous strip. Press seam in either direction. From this cut 1 – 2" x 60 1/2" strip. Sew to left hand side of quilt center. Press toward border.

2. Right hand border:
   Sew black texture 4 1/2" black texture strips end-to-end to make one continuous strip. Press seam in either direction. From this cut 1 – 4 1/2" x 60 1/2" strip. Sew to right hand side of quilt center. Press toward border.

3. Top inner border:
   Sew the two remaining black texture 2" x wof strips end-to-end to make one continuous strip. Press seam in either direction. From this cut 1 – 2" x 51" strip. Sew to top of quilt center. Press to border.

4. Left hand outer border:
   Sew white stripe 4 1/2" x wof strips end to end to make one continuous strip. Press seam in either direction. From this cut 1 – 4 1/2" x 62" strip. Sew to left hand side of quilt center. Press to border.

5. Bottom Border:
   Sew black floral 4 1/2" strips end to end to make one continuous strip. Press seam in either direction. From this cut 1 – 4 1/2" x 55 1/2" strip. Sew to bottom of quilt center. Press to border.

6. Top Border:
   Sew multi-color dot 4 1/2" x wof strips end to end to make one continuous strip. Press seam in either direction. From this cut 1 – 4 1/2" x 55 1/2" strip. Sew to top of quilt center. Press to border.

Single Flower

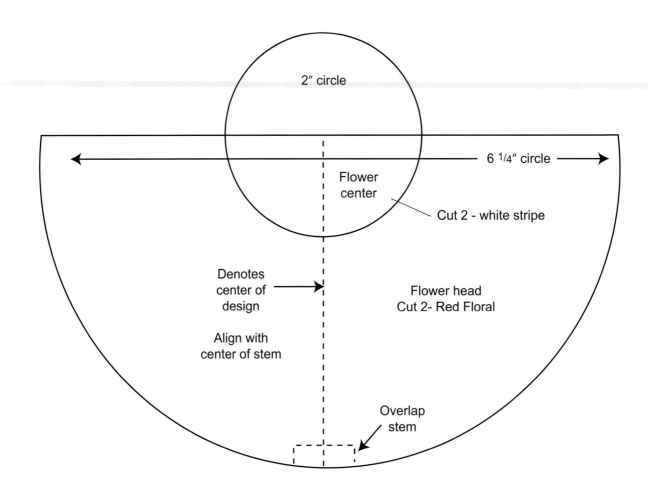

2" circle

6 1/4" circle

Flower
center

Cut 2 - white stripe

Denotes
center of
design

Flower head
Cut 2- Red Floral

Align with
center of stem

Overlap
stem

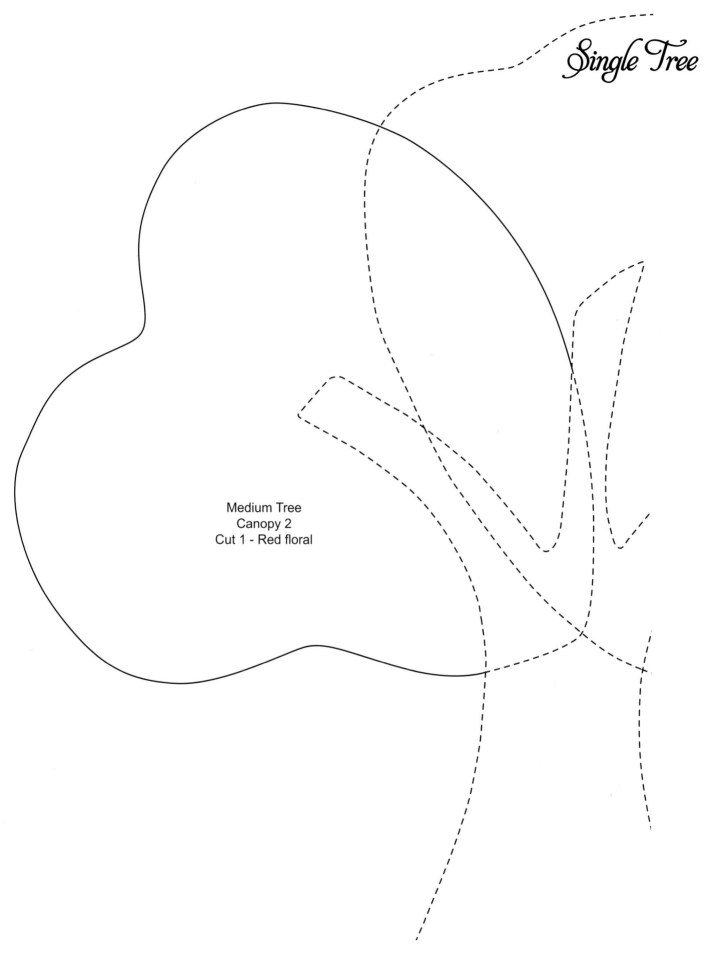

Medium Tree
Canopy 2
Cut 1 - Red floral

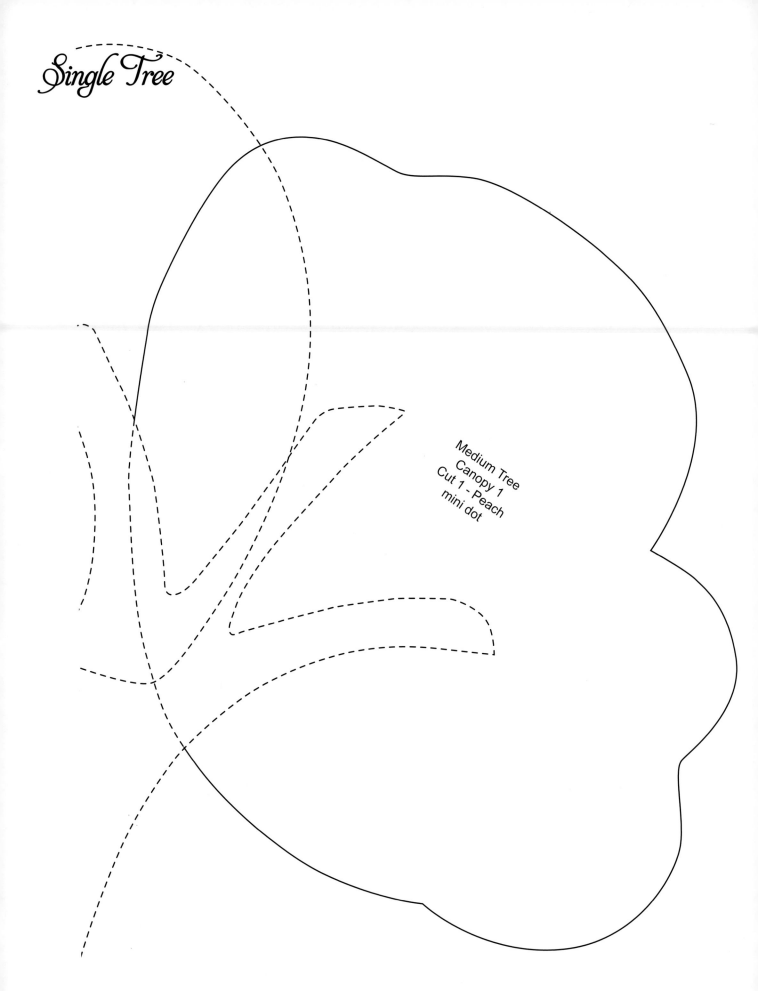

Single Tree

Medium Tree
Canopy 1
Cut 1 - Peach
mini dot

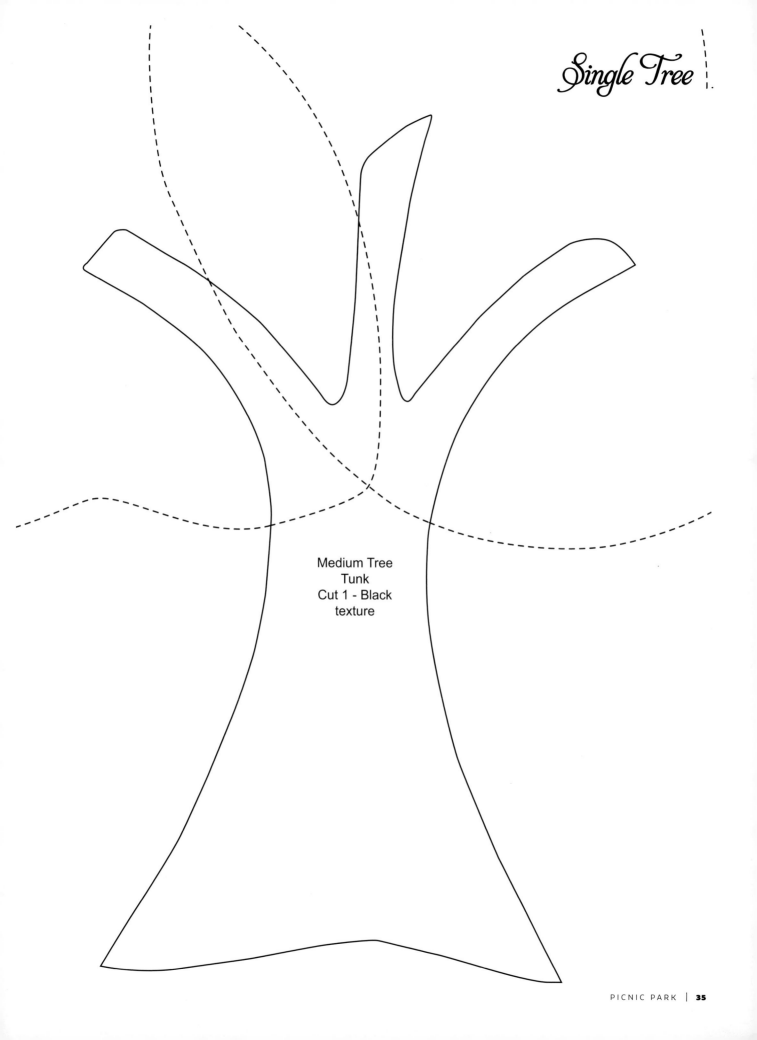

Medium Tree
Tunk
Cut 1 - Black
texture

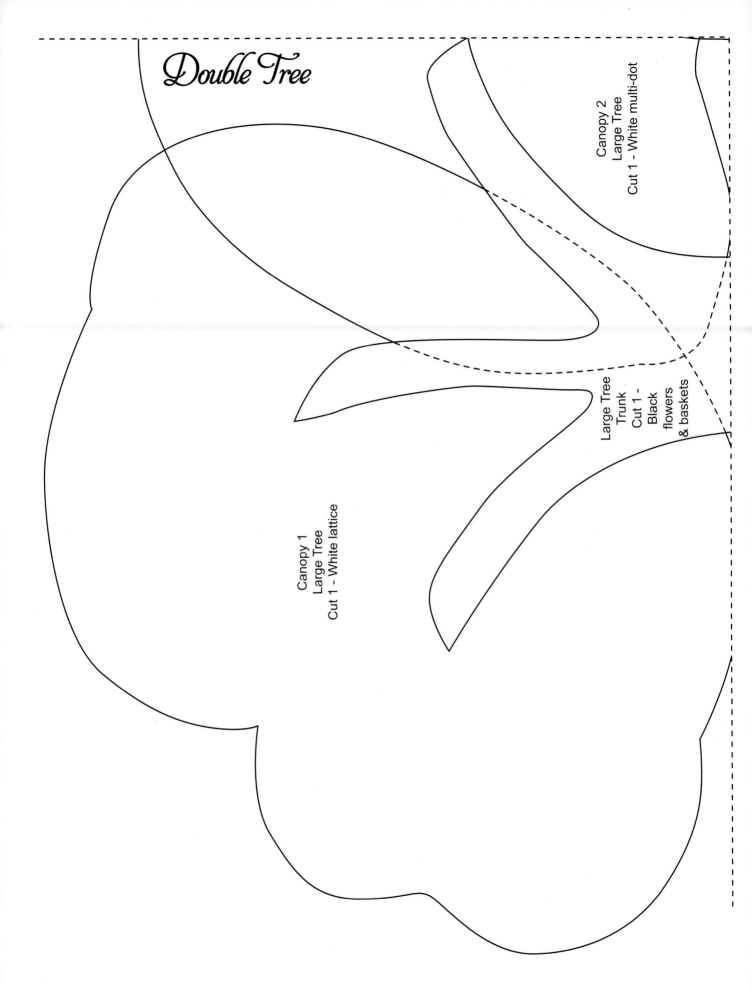

Double Tree

Canopy 2
Large Tree
Cut 1 - White multi-dot

Large Tree
Trunk
Cut 1 -
Black
flowers
& baskets

Canopy 1
Large Tree
Cut 1 - White lattice

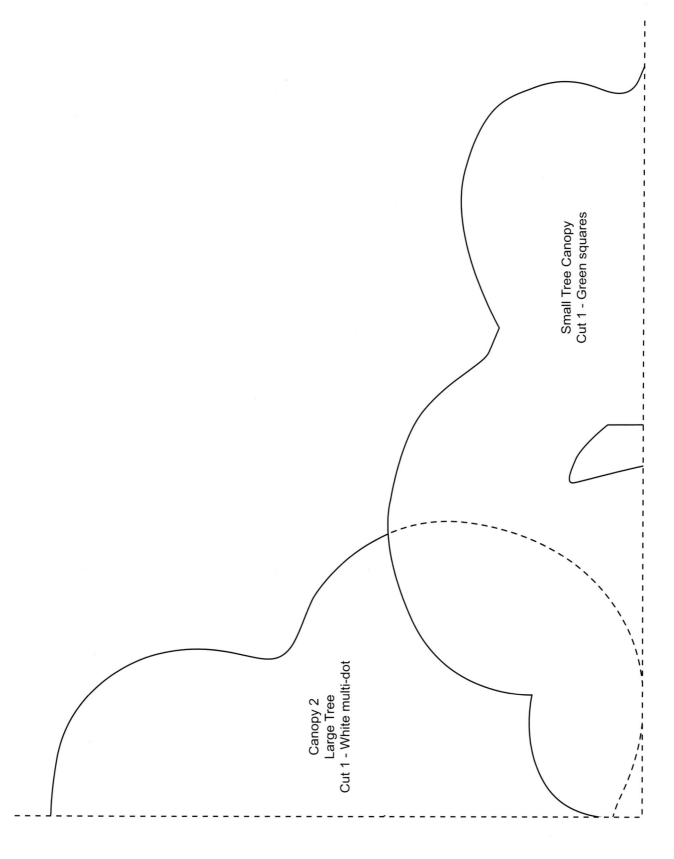

Small Tree Canopy
Cut 1 - Green squares

Canopy 2
Large Tree
Cut 1 - White multi-dot

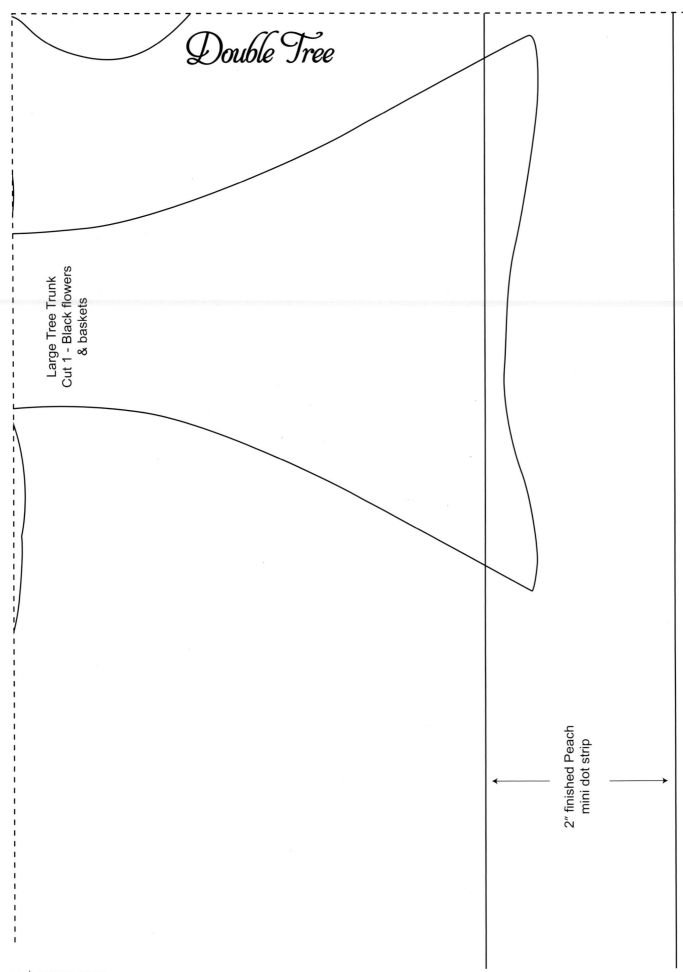

Double Tree

Large Tree Trunk
Cut 1 - Black flowers
& baskets

2" finished Peach
mini dot strip

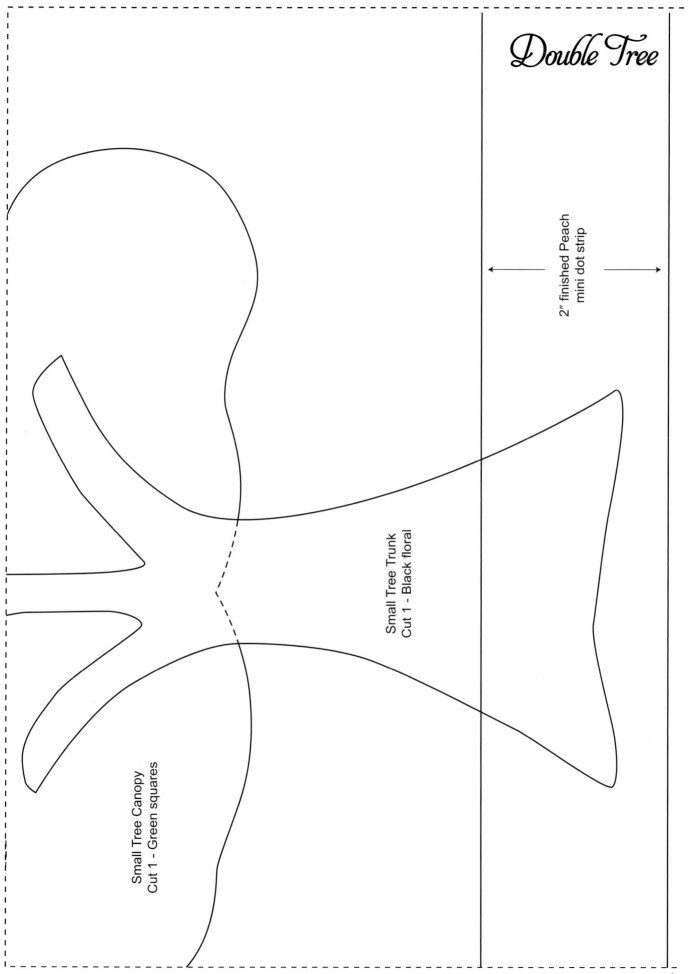

2" finished Peach mini dot strip

Small Tree Trunk
Cut 1 - Black floral

Small Tree Canopy
Cut 1 - Green squares

Big Watermelon

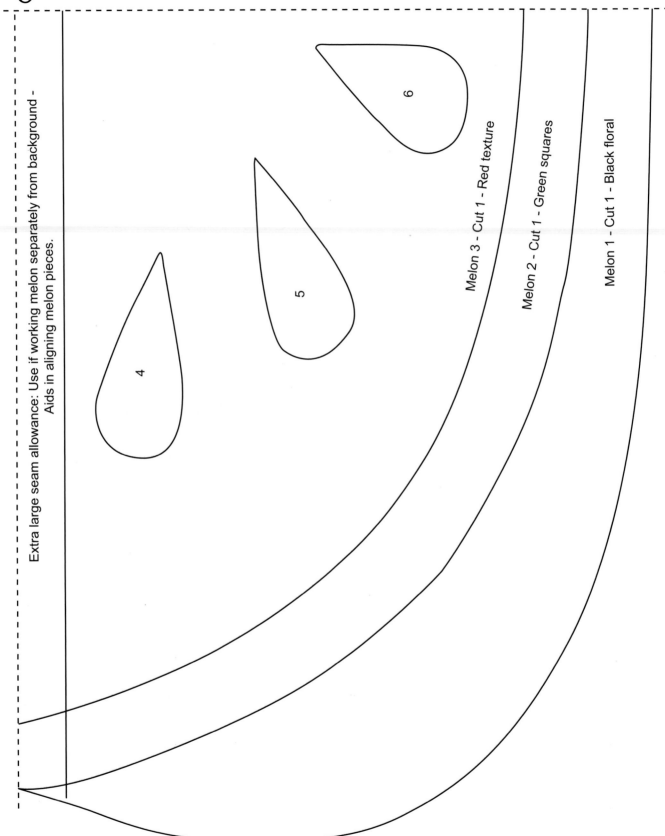

Extra large seam allowance: Use if working melon separately from background - Aids in aligning melon pieces.

4

5

6

Melon 3 - Cut 1 - Red texture

Melon 2 - Cut 1 - Green squares

Melon 1 - Cut 1 - Black floral

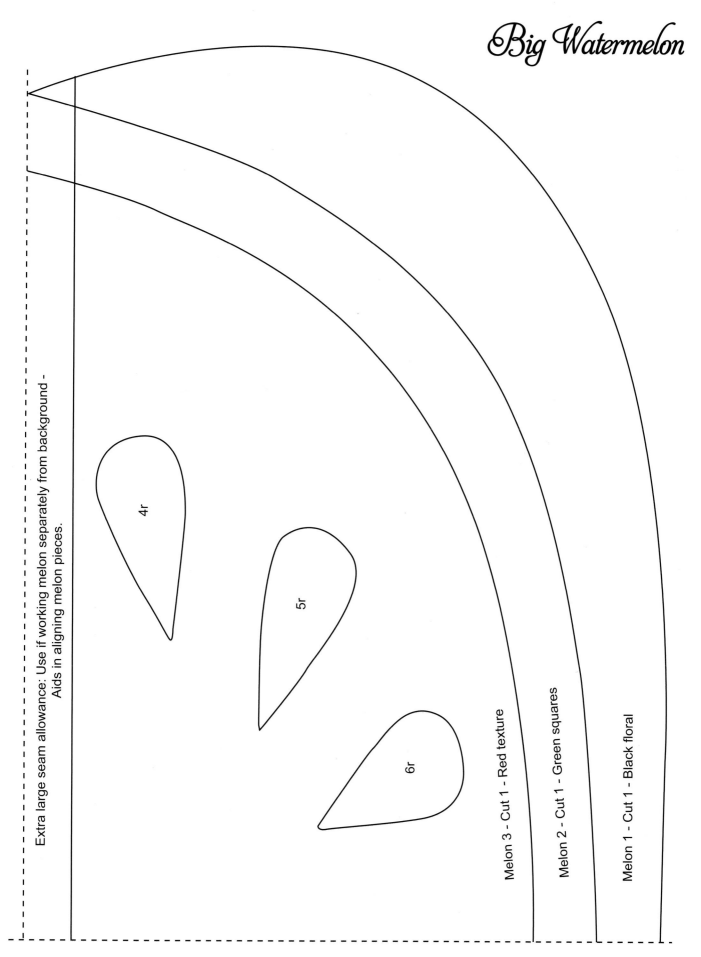

Big Watermelon

Extra large seam allowance: Use if working melon separately from background - Aids in aligning melon pieces.

4r

5r

6r

Melon 3 - Cut 1 - Red texture

Melon 2 - Cut 1 - Green squares

Melon 1 - Cut 1 - Black floral

Picnic Basket

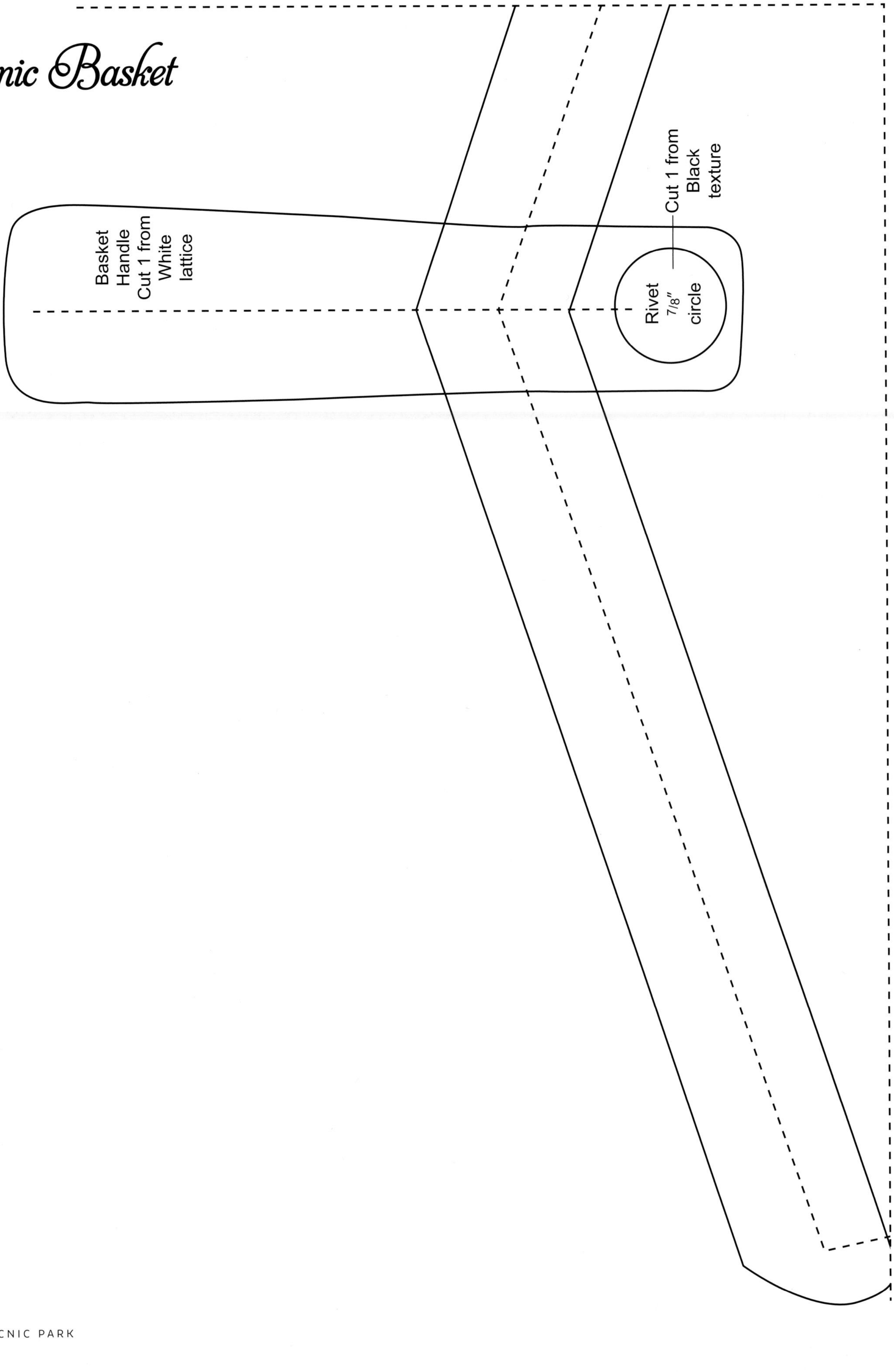

Basket
Handle
Cut 1 from
White
lattice

Cut 1 from
Black
texture

Rivet
7/8"
circle

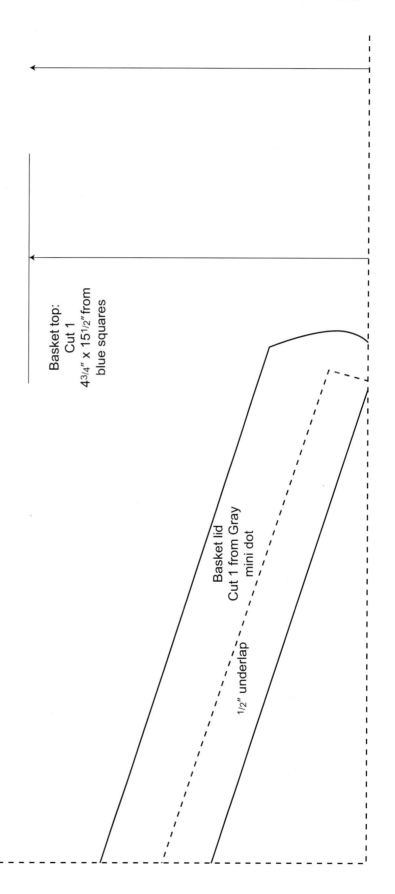

Basket top:
Cut 1
4³/₄" x 15¹/₂" from
blue squares

Basket lid
Cut 1 from Gray
mini dot

¹/₂" underlap

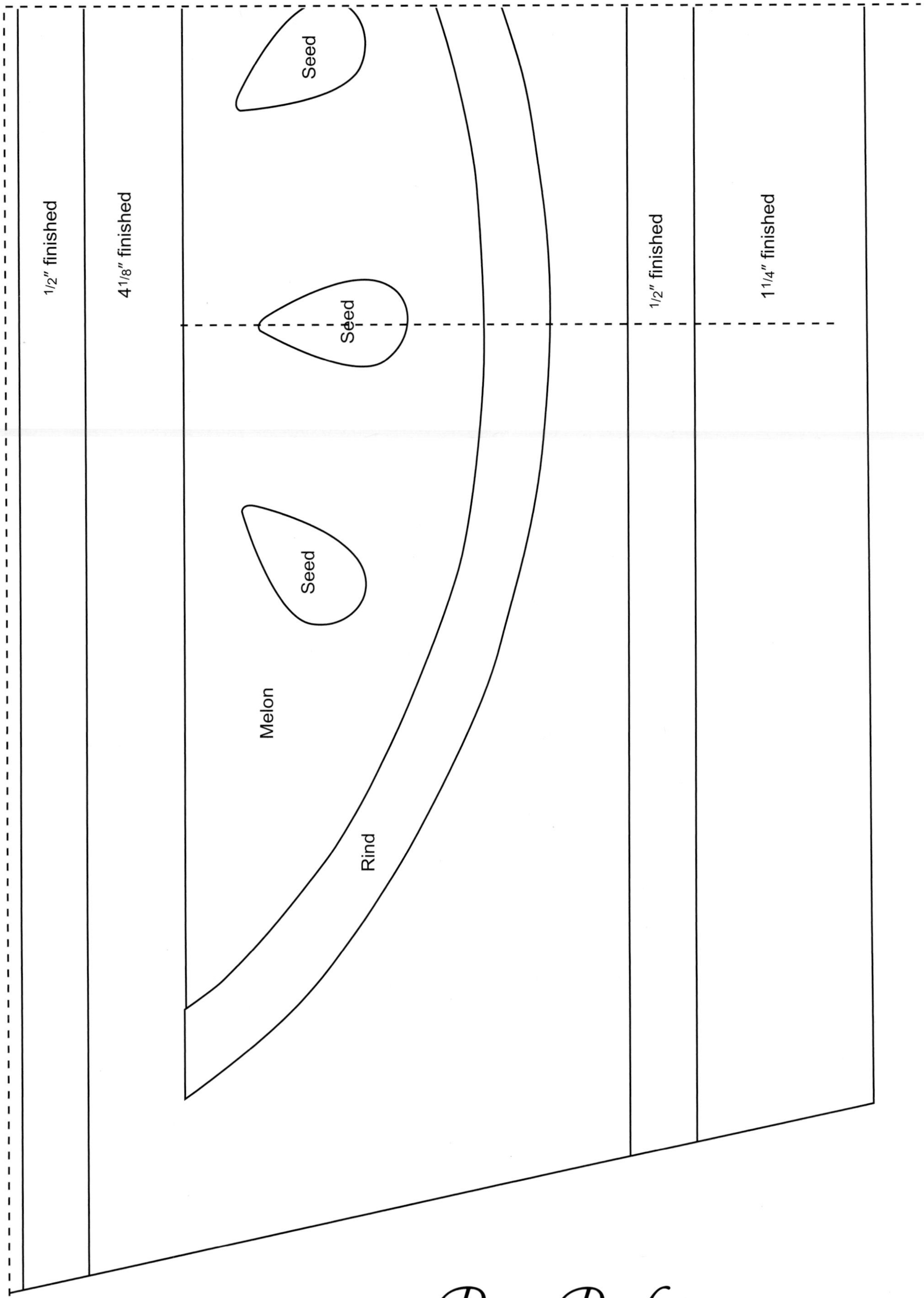

½" finished

4⅛" finished

Seed

Seed
Seed

Seed

Melon

Rind

½" finished

1¼" finished

Picnic Basket

Prepare freezer paper pattern for complete basket

Mark stripes on paper pattern

Basket stripe
Gray mini dot

Cut 2
1" x 15½"

Watermelon
Panel
Cut 1
5⅝" x 15½"
White lattice

Basket
stripe

Basket
bottom:
Cut 1
2¼" x 15½"
from Blue
squares

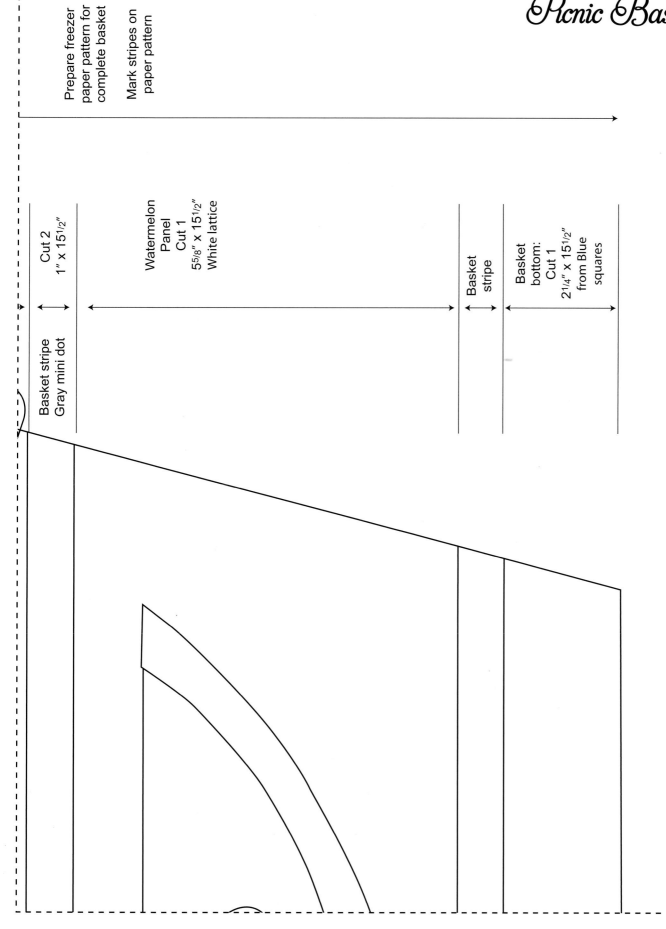

Tumbler

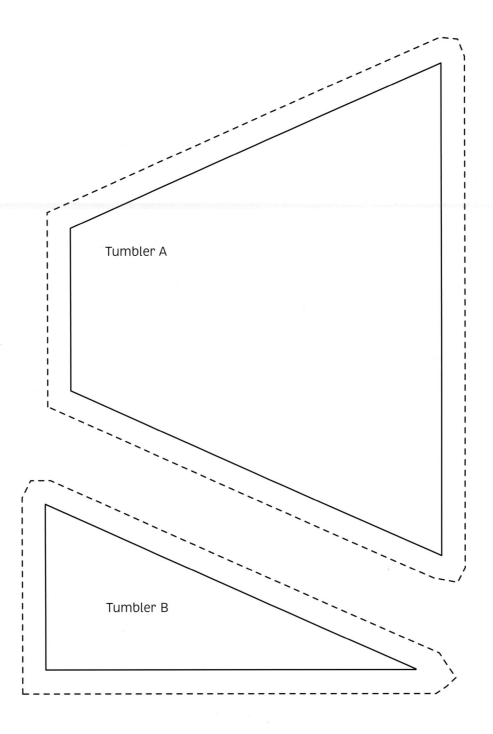

Tumbler A

Tumbler B

Flower Basket

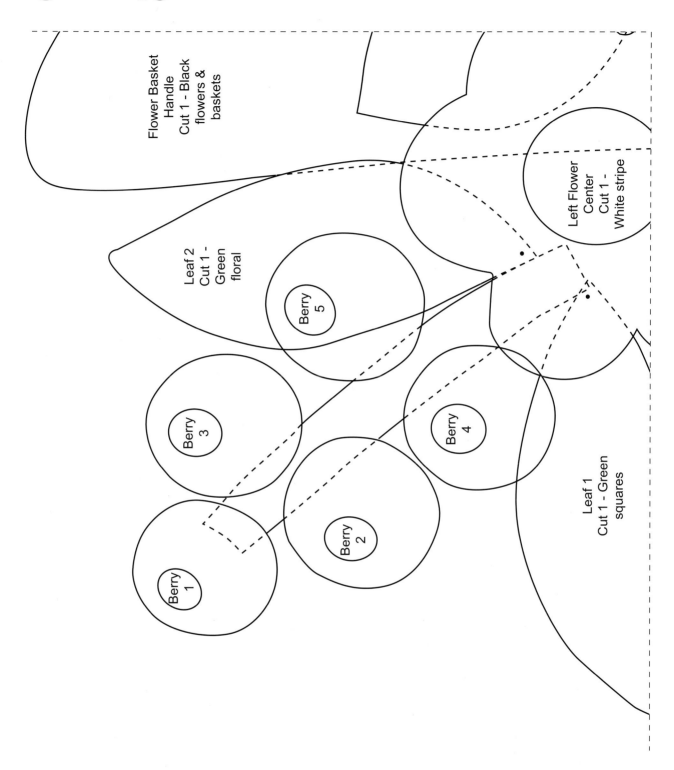

Flower Basket
Handle
Cut 1 - Black
flowers &
baskets

Left Flower
Center
Cut 1 -
White stripe

Leaf 2
Cut 1 -
Green
floral

Berry
5

Berry
3

Berry
4

Berry
1

Berry
2

Leaf 1
Cut 1 - Green
squares

Flower Basket

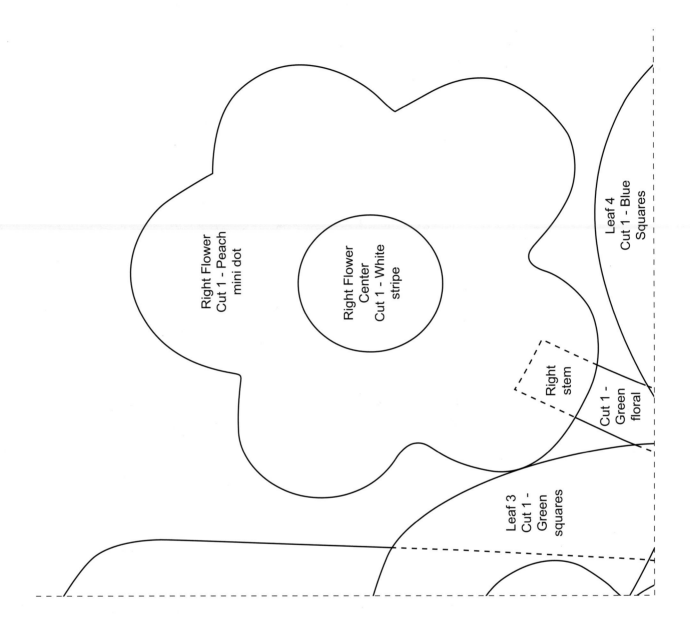

Right Flower
Cut 1 - Peach
mini dot

Right Flower
Center
Cut 1 - White
stripe

Leaf 4
Cut 1 - Blue
Squares

Right
stem

Cut 1 -
Green
floral

Leaf 3
Cut 1 -
Green
squares

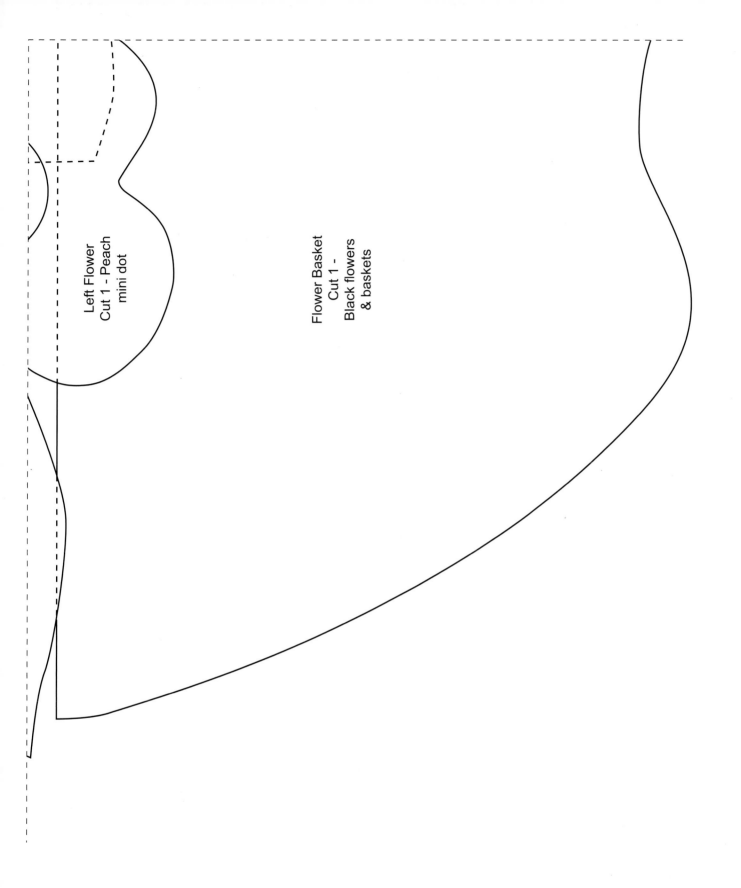

Left Flower
Cut 1 - Peach
mini dot

Flower Basket
Cut 1 -
Black flowers
& baskets

Flower Basket

Flower Basket

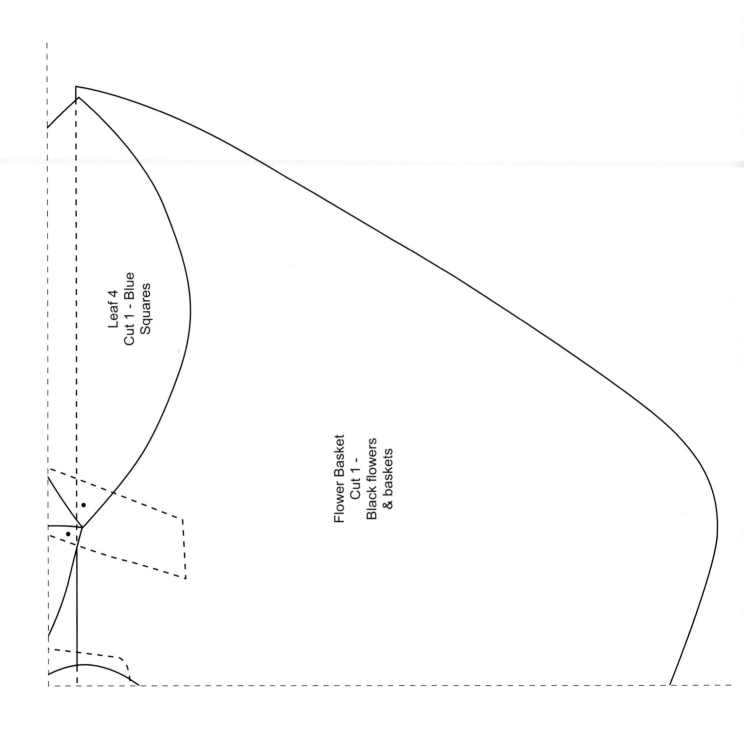

Leaf 4
Cut 1 - Blue
Squares

Flower Basket
Cut 1 -
Black flowers
& baskets

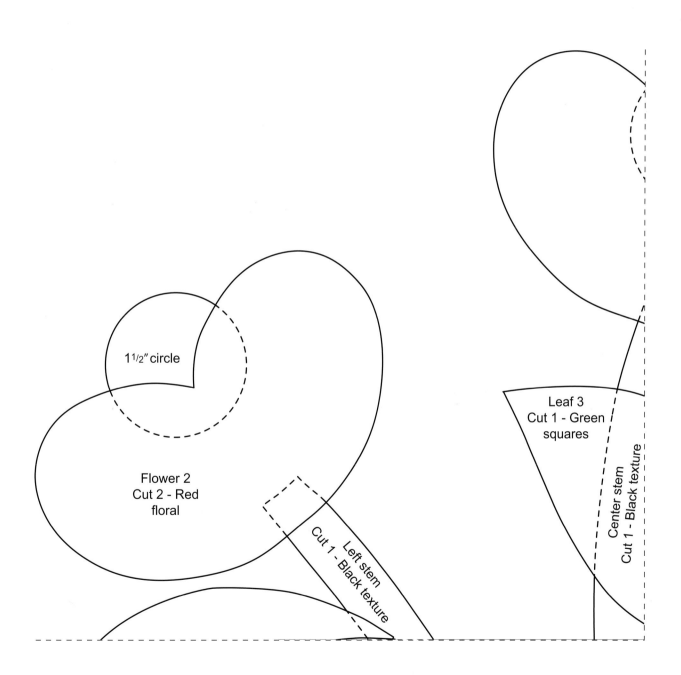

1¹/₂″ circle

Flower 2
Cut 2 - Red
floral

Left stem
Cut 1 - Black texture

Leaf 3
Cut 1 - Green
squares

Center stem
Cut 1 - Black texture

Flower Pot

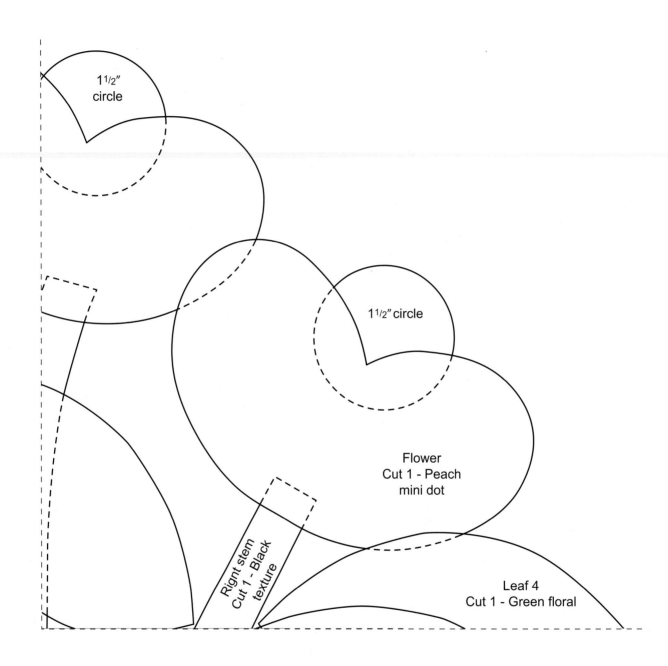

1½" circle

1½" circle

Flower
Cut 1 - Peach
mini dot

Right stem
Cut 1 - Black
texture

Leaf 4
Cut 1 - Green floral

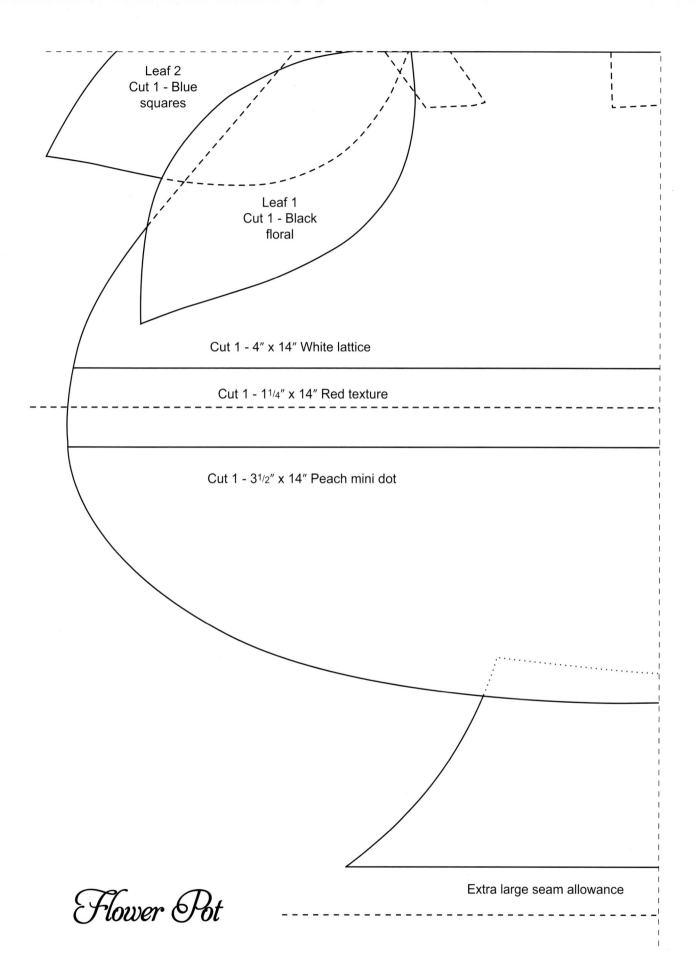

Leaf 2
Cut 1 - Blue
squares

Leaf 1
Cut 1 - Black
floral

Cut 1 - 4″ x 14″ White lattice

Cut 1 - 1¼″ x 14″ Red texture

Cut 1 - 3½″ x 14″ Peach mini dot

Extra large seam allowance

Flower Pot

Flower Pot

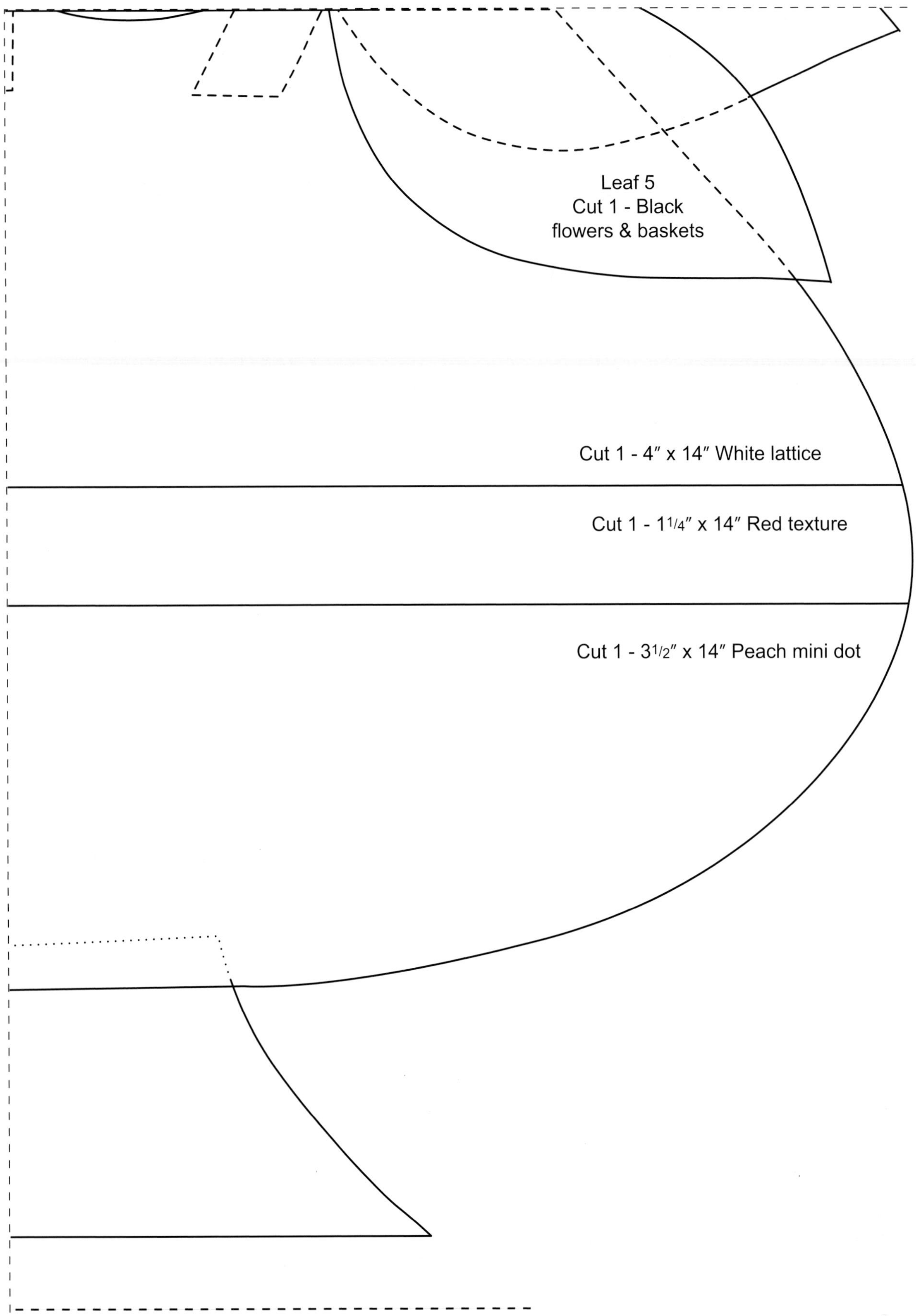

Leaf 5
Cut 1 - Black
flowers & baskets

Cut 1 - 4″ x 14″ White lattice

Cut 1 - 1¼″ x 14″ Red texture

Cut 1 - 3½″ x 14″ Peach mini dot